BY:

# SUSAN LA FLESCHE PICOTTE

**Discover history's heroes
and their stories.**

*Dennis Brutus*

*Michael Collins*

*Ida B. Wells*

# DISCOVERING HISTORY'S
# HEROES
## SUSAN LA FLESCHE PICOTTE

## BY DIANE BAILEY

Aladdin
New York   London   Toronto   Sydney   New Delhi

ALADDIN

An imprint of Simon & Schuster Children's Publishing Division
1230 Avenue of the Americas, New York, New York 10020
First Aladdin hardcover edition May 2021
Text copyright © 2021 by Diane Bailey
Jacket illustration copyright © 2021 by Lisa K. Weber
Also available in an Aladdin paperback edition.

For information about special discounts for bulk purchases,
please contact Simon & Schuster Special Sales at
1-866-506-1949 or business@simonandschuster.com.
The Simon & Schuster Speakers Bureau can bring authors to your live
event. For more information or to book an event contact the
Simon & Schuster Speakers Bureau at 1-866-248-3049
or visit our website at www.simonspeakers.com.
Jacket designed by Heather Palisi
Interior designed by Mike Rosamilia
The text of this book was set in Adobe Caslon Pro.
Manufactured in the United States of America 0321 FFG
2 4 6 8 10 9 7 5 3 1
Library of Congress Control Number 2020949300
ISBN 978-1-5344-6331-8 (hc)
ISBN 978-1-5344-6330-1 (pbk)
ISBN 978-1-5344-6332-5 (eBook)

# CONTENTS

# A NOTE TO THE READER

Several different terms are used to describe Susan La Flesche Picotte, the people in the Omaha tribe she belonged to, and other native peoples who first lived in America. In Susan's time the word "Indian" was common. That's because when the Italian explorer Christopher Columbus first landed in America, he actually thought he was in the country of India. He called the people he saw "Indians," and the name stuck. Later the name became "American Indian," a term that is still widely used today (even though America is very far away from India!).

Some people prefer to say "Native American." They feel this better describes the people who were the first to live in the Americas, long before European settlers arrived. However, the phrase "Native American" also comes from Europeans, since it was Europeans who came up with the name "America." That's why other people like to use the term "indigenous peoples." "Indigenous," which means "native," describes the first peoples without using a word that European settlers introduced.

As for Susan, she grew up hearing the word "Indian," both among her Omaha tribe and from whites. Since that is how she described herself and her people, the terms "Indian" and "Native American" are used in this book.

## Prologue
# A PLEA FOR HELP

The Omaha woman lay in bed, weak and frail. She was getting sicker and sicker. Her family sent for the doctor, a white man who was in charge of helping the Indians in the Omaha tribe. Please come quickly, they begged. The doctor sent his answer: he would come. The family breathed a sigh of relief. And then they waited.

Susan La Flesche was worried about the woman, but she was just a little girl. There wasn't much she could do to help except sit beside the older woman, straighten her covers, and give her sips of water to soothe her parched lips. She could hold the woman's hand and try to comfort her. But it wasn't enough. The woman needed a doctor. What was taking him so long?

As the hours passed and the doctor still did not show up, another message was sent. The woman was getting worse, and she was in terrible pain. Time was running out. She needed help *now*. Again, the doctor assured them that he was on his way—and again, he didn't come.

Twice more during the night, urgent messages flew across the Nebraska plains to the doctor. Four times altogether. Each time he promised to come, but he never did.

The next morning the woman died.

Susan was angry with the doctor. His job was to help sick, suffering people—but he hadn't bothered to help the Omaha woman who'd needed him. To him it wasn't important that the woman had died.

She'd been "only an Indian," Susan said later, and "[did] not matter."[1]

But the woman had mattered, of course. She'd mattered to her family and her tribe. And she'd mattered to Susan. Susan remembered that sad night for the rest of her life. She promised herself that if she ever got the chance, she wouldn't let people suffer. Not if she could help them. And she *would* find a way to help them.

That was what mattered.

Susan was an Omaha Indian who lived in the late 1800s and early 1900s. She devoted her life to helping her people however she could. Along the way, she faced a lot of obstacles, but she didn't get discouraged. She looked for a path around each obstacle—and she usually found one! When Susan was born, the lives of the Omaha were changing fast. Sometimes it was difficult, but Susan was optimistic. She believed that good things could come from those changes. She was always looking toward the future—but she never forgot her past.

Her goal was to make the lives of the Omaha better. As the country's first Native American to earn a medical degree, she used her skills to improve their health. She also worked for them to have more rights in a country that sometimes did not treat them well. She didn't always succeed, but throughout her life, she showed how determination and kindness could change lives.

# 1.
# BORN WITH THE BUFFALO

In June 1865, the Omaha Indians were on the move. They had planted their crops, and in the fall the tribe would return to their **reservation** to harvest corn, squash, beans, and melons. For a few weeks during the summer, though, they were traveling across the plains, camping in their teepees, hunting for buffalo. The Omaha way of life depended on the buffalo. The animals' meat would feed the tribe through the winter, and their furry coats would become warm blankets and robes. Their skin was turned into moccasins and teepee coverings.

In the past, millions of buffalo had roamed the Nebraska prairie. But those herds were dwindling as white men moved into the Great Plains and killed the buffalo. Sometimes it was for food, but more often it was just for sport. Joseph La Flesche, who was also called "Iron Eye," was chief of the Omaha tribe. He feared there weren't many years left when his people would be able to go on their annual summer hunt. What would happen then?

As these problems stood before the Omaha, though, good news spread through the camp. On June 17, Iron Eye's wife Mary (also known as "One Woman") gave birth to a baby girl. For a little while Joseph set aside his worries. Right now it was time to greet his new daughter.

Susan La Flesche was born into a big, close family. She already had three older sisters: Susette was eleven, Rosalie was four, and Marguerite was three. (A brother, Louis, had been born in 1848 but had died.)

Joseph also had a second wife, which was common

among the Omaha people. From this marriage Susan had a half brother named Francis, who was seven when Susan was born. Her half sister, Lucy, was born the same year as Susan. Another half brother, Carey, came in 1872, the year Susan turned seven.

As soon as she was old enough, Susan was expected to help the family in any way she could. She learned how to plant and harvest crops, and how to dry strips of buffalo meat.

One of her jobs was to carry water from the spring to the house. Susan dreaded that chore! It was a long walk, barefoot over the rough grass, with the sun beating down on her back. And the buckets were heavy!

But there was plenty of time to play, too. Everyone laughed during the dance of the turkeys, when the children imitated the funny way turkeys poked their necks out. Other times the kids stared at one another until someone cracked a smile. Whoever smiled first lost the game—and got water poured over their head. Susan and her sisters played house in teepees that they built, taking care of dolls made from corncobs and dressed in bits of calico fabric. The sisters rode across the Nebraska prairie on stick ponies they made from the tall stalks of sunflowers.

Like all other Omaha children, Susan behaved respectfully around her parents and other adults. She knew it was rude to walk in between a person and the flap of the tent, and she knew not to stare at people—especially strangers! She learned to get up quietly, without drawing attention to herself. Of course she never interrupted when the grown-ups were talking. And from the time Susan was a little girl, the grown-ups were always talking. Big changes were happening on the reservation, and more changes were coming.

Joseph had become chief of the Omaha in 1853. By then, thousands of white people had been moving onto Indian lands. Joseph had seen how the US government had helped these settlers take over the land of other Indian tribes. He knew that the United States wanted the Omaha's land too. Joseph worried that if the Omaha did not **surrender** their land voluntarily, the US government might take it by force. The Omaha were a small tribe, and not very powerful. They would not be able to stop the strong US military.

Joseph believed that for his tribe to have a peaceful, productive future, they needed to find a way to live alongside white men—not fight against them. So in 1854 he signed a **treaty** between the Omaha and the US government. Under the agreement, the Omaha sold the United States millions of acres of land that were their traditional hunting lands. In return, the Omaha got to keep living on a small piece of land, about 300,000 acres, that was nestled on the banks of the Missouri River in northeastern Nebraska. This was now the Omaha reservation.

However, the US government made sure they had a lot of power over the Omaha. The treaty made it clear that the Omaha were to use their reservation land in ways that white men approved of—namely, farming.

Although the Omaha were used to raising a few crops, the US government wanted them to take up full-time, large-scale farming, like white men did. According to the treaty, the government didn't even have to pay the Omaha the money they were owed from the sale of their hunting grounds. Instead, the United States could decide to use the money on programs for the "moral improvement and education" of the Omaha, or for starting farms and buying supplies. In return, the government helped the Omaha set up a mill, for grinding corn and flour, and a blacksmith shop to take care of their equipment. Finally, the US military promised to protect the Omaha from other Indian tribes such as the Sioux, who had been enemies of the Omaha for a long time. To make sure things were done the way the US government wanted, officials established an office on the reservation, called an agency, to take care of things.

Many of the Omaha opposed Joseph's decision to cooperate with the United States. He had sold almost all the Omaha's lands. How could they go on their annual hunts, which were so important to the tribe? Joseph sympathized with them, but he was their chief. He insisted that he'd done the right thing.

Joseph started to adopt the ways of white men. In the past the Omaha had lived in earth lodges or teepees. But white men lived in wooden houses with square corners and glass panes in the windows. In 1857, Joseph built a wooden house for his family. It was the first one on the reservation. He planted crops and kept cattle, just like white men. He also joined the Presbyterian Church, which established a **mission** on the reservation to spread the Christian religion among the Indians. Some Omaha followed Joseph's lead and built their own wooden houses. But others refused. They mocked what they called the Village of the Make-Believe White Men.

Joseph was proud of his Indian heritage, and he wanted his children to be proud of it too. But he also wanted them to fit into the white man's world. That meant making some changes. For example, Joseph and

Mary gave their oldest daughter a traditional Indian name that meant "Bright Eyes," but they also gave her an English name, Susette. The rest of the children, including Susan, got only English names. Because Susan and her sisters were daughters of a chief, normally they would have received tattoos to show their status. Not now. Joseph did not want them to look different.

Still, Susan grew up knowing how to speak Omaha as well as English, and understanding the traditions of her people. Many evenings her grandmother would come by the house and tell a story. Susan loved to listen to funny tales of rabbits who played tricks, or to silly explanations for why turkeys have red eyes. Sometimes the stories had a message. The Omaha were patient, cautious people. They did not rush into things. The stories explained that before making a big decision, "the people thought."[2]

And so Susan grew up with a foot in two worlds—one Omaha, one white.

Both of them made her think.

# 2.
# FROM PRAIRIE TO COAST

*Shhhh.* . . . Gently the big boys picked Susan up. Her dark hair, twisted into braids, hung down as the boys lifted her out of her seat and laid her down inside a school desk. They weren't being mean, though. Susan was fast asleep! The boys were just tucking her away somewhere nice and quiet.

When she started going to the Presbyterian mission school on the reservation, Susan was only about three years old. It was no wonder she sometimes needed a nap before the day was finished. And the teacher didn't seem to think class was very important anyway. Sometimes he put a newspaper over his head, leaned back in his chair, and nodded off himself. Susan later remembered, "I can't say as I learned very much."[3]

About a year later the Presbyterian school closed and Susan transferred to another school on the reservation. In the mornings she and her sisters Rosalie and Marguerite met up with fifteen or twenty other kids. They swung their tin lunch pails as they walked the three miles to school. It would have been fun to stop and pick flowers or chase butterflies, but Susan did not get distracted. Even as a child, she was always focused and disciplined. When school started at nine a.m., Susan was at her desk, ready to tackle her reading, writing, and arithmetic.

A few years later Susan's older sister Susette got a job teaching at the school and moved into a small house nearby. Susan, Marguerite, and Rosalie all moved in with her. Now they did not have to walk so far to school each day.

When she'd lived at home, Susan had spoken French and Omaha with her parents. But Joseph actually wanted his daughters to speak only English, and Susette agreed with her father. If Susette's younger sisters spoke to her in Omaha, she ignored them. At first Susette didn't hear much out of Susan, because her English wasn't very good. But Susan's options were to speak English or not at all, so she learned fast!

All the girls worked together to keep house. Susette was the oldest, but she had no intention of doing all the work herself. She already had a full-time job! She made sure all of her sisters helped with the chores. As the youngest, Susan got odd jobs like cleaning knives and beating eggs. In the evenings Susette read out loud to her younger sisters as they sewed their dresses. One of their favorite things to listen to was *St. Nicholas Magazine*, a popular children's magazine with stories, drawings, and puzzles that were often submitted by children.

In 1877, when Susan was twelve, she and her sisters decided to write letters to the magazine. In her letter Susan proudly reported that she was reading in the Fifth Reader. That referred to McGuffey's **Eclectic** Readers, a set of books that most children of the time learned from. The first book in the series was very easy, with sentences like "Ann has a fan" and "Nat has a hat." Since Susan was up to the Fifth Reader, the reading was much harder—but it was also a lot more interesting than reading about Ann and Nat (who ran and sat).

By the time she was fourteen, Susan had learned all she could at the reservation school. Years earlier her sister Susette had gone to the Elizabeth Institute for Young Ladies, which was in New Jersey. Now Joseph thought it was time for Susan and Marguerite to go as well. The school was all the way across the country, more than a thousand miles away. Susan wasn't sure whether to be excited or scared!

She was nervous about leaving her home, her family, and her friends. She would be gone for three years. During that time, she wouldn't be able to ride her beloved pony across the prairie, or listen to her grandmother's stories. She could forget about wearing a comfortable pair of moccasins around the house. For three years she'd be stuck wearing the stiff shoes that white people wore. Just thinking about it probably made her feet hurt.

She would still study reading, writing, and math, just like she had on the reservation—but there would be more of it, and it would be more difficult. But maybe she'd get to try new things too. Maybe she'd get to read great works of literature. Maybe she'd learn some science.

Once, when she was six years old, Joseph had said to Susan and her sisters, "My dear young daughters, do you always want to be simply called 'those Indians,' or do you want to go to school and be somebody in the world?"[4]

Well, Susan knew the answer to that question! "From that moment, I determined to make something useful of myself," she later wrote.[5]

When Susan traveled to the school in New Jersey, she was not yet grown up, but she was not a little girl anymore either. If she was going to "be somebody," she had to take chances—even if they did feel a little scary.

The Elizabeth Institute was a big change from what Susan was used to, but she and Marguerite quickly settled in. Susan dived into her classes in literature, math, and philosophy. The institute was also a finishing school. The idea was that young women would "finish" their formal education by learning proper **etiquette** and how to behave respectably in society.

Over the next three years Susan got a good education, but she missed her family. When she and Marguerite finished their schooling in the spring of 1882, Susan was excited to go home.

By now her English was perfect (and so were her manners). When she first returned to the reservation, Susan tried being a seamstress, but it turned out that she was much better at school than at sewing. Soon she began teaching a class for young children at the mission school, which had reopened a few years earlier. The mission building was the center of reservation life, and Susan liked being in the middle of things. People were always going in and out on various errands. It was a busy place!

One day it got even busier.

# 3.
# AN IMPORTANT FRIEND

Francis La Flesche's horse-drawn wagon raced into the yard of the mission school one afternoon in July 1883. The wheels flung up mud from the recent rainstorm. Susan's half brother jumped down from the driver's seat and circled around to the back of the wagon. There a woman was lying on a cot. Susan knew that woman: it was Alice Fletcher. Something must have been very wrong!

Alice was a white woman and a good friend of the La Flesche family. She was an **ethnologist**, a scholar who studied the history and customs of various groups of people. She was particularly interested in the Omaha. Alice had lived in Massachusetts and had met Susan's brother Francis and sister Susette when they'd been traveling in the East. The three had become friends.

Alice had wanted to move to the Omaha reservation so she could live among the people and learn about them firsthand. She'd asked Francis and Susette to help her, and they'd agreed.

Alice arrived at the reservation in the early 1880s. At the time, Joseph La Flesche was still working to get the Omaha to adapt to the ways of white men. He wanted the Indians to learn to speak English and become farmers. Now he also supported a plan by the US government to give the Omaha tribe members **land allotments** taken from the reservation land. These were individual pieces of land that they could use to farm.

Owning private pieces of property was very

common among white people, but it was strange to the Omaha. How could anyone *own* the land? That made no sense to them. In their way of life they managed large areas of land together, as a tribe. Everyone shared.

Now the US government said they had to do things differently. However, the government didn't trust the Omaha to adjust to the new system without any problems. Whites did not understand Indians very well at all. Many whites thought that Indians were irresponsible and even lazy. So the government wanted to be sure each Omaha who received a piece of land knew how to take care of it *before* they truly owned it. To do this, the government decided to set up twenty-five-year **trust**s. That meant that the people who received the allotments could live on and use the land but could not sell it for twenty-five years. At the end of the twenty-five years, the US government would review how things had gone. If the government agents decided that the people using the land had done everything right, the land would officially become theirs.

It was a poor way to treat people who had lived on the land for centuries and had done fine by themselves. Nonetheless, Joseph and many other Omaha felt that they had to agree to the twenty-five-year trusts. The Omaha had seen the US government seize land from other Indian tribes and didn't want the same thing to happen to them. They hoped that owning the land as private individuals would protect them.

Alice liked the Omaha people and wanted to help them. Like Joseph, she supported the allotment plan, which became a law in 1882. All of this meant a lot of paperwork! Alice was working day and night to help the Omaha people understand the new policy and fill out the correct forms.

That was what she was doing when she got caught in the storm in July 1883. The rain soaked her to the skin, but it was a warm summer day, so at first she didn't worry about it. She was so busy working that she didn't even stop to peel off her wet clothes and put on dry ones. That turned out to be a big mistake! Her clothes soon got cold, and it wasn't long before Alice's whole body was cold too. Her muscles stiffened up. After a few hours Alice was absolutely miserable. She realized she was in trouble and sent word to Francis for help. When he arrived, he saw that Alice could barely move. Quickly he helped her into the back of the wagon and started on the thirty-mile drive to the mission school.

By the time they reached the school, Alice was terribly sick. She was chilled to the bone. Her arms hurt. Her legs hurt. Her neck and hips and fingers hurt. *Everything* hurt. Alice suffered from something called inflammatory rheumatism, which made her joints swell up. She was in awful pain. Unfortunately, she did not feel better as soon as she warmed up. For three weeks she could not even get out of bed. She was so sick that many people thought she would die.

Alice was lucky, though. She had Susan taking care of her. Susan brought Alice her meals and made sure she got her medicine. Susan sat by her bedside and chatted with her to help pass the hours. Alice was so grateful.

It took months for her to recover, and Susan helped her during that long, slow period. Susan was kind and attentive—the perfect nurse! But Alice also saw that Susan was curious, intelligent, and eager to learn. Susan's time at the Elizabeth Institute had turned her into a young woman who was more educated than many others on the Omaha reservation. Alice thought Susan could do big things with her life if she kept up with her education.

Even better, Alice knew just the place to make that happen!

The Hampton Normal and Agricultural Institute was located on the coast of Chesapeake Bay in Virginia. It had been started in 1868 by Samuel Armstrong, an army general who had led Black troops during the

Civil War. After the war had ended, he'd wanted to help former slaves get an education. Before the war, most Black people in the South had been slaves. In some places it had actually been illegal for them to go to school! After slaves became free, they still faced problems. Many whites felt **prejudice** against them. Most Blacks could not read or write, and it was difficult for them to find good jobs.

General Armstrong wanted to give African Americans the chance to learn practical skills and to develop good character. They would pay for their education by working. Then they would be ready to lead productive lives in white society.

General Armstrong's attitude was common at the time. He had good intentions, but like many other white people, he thought Blacks had to be taught that education and hard work were important. He believed they could be useful and productive only if white people helped them, and only if they did things the same way whites did.

At first Hampton admitted only Black students, but in 1878, General Armstrong decided to expand the school so that Indians could also attend. His opinion of Indians was similar to what he thought of Blacks. He believed they did not understand the value of education and working for a living. Again, he hoped this new group of students would also learn to adapt to white ways.

Hampton was one of few schools that welcomed Indians, so as soon as Alice had her strength back, she started writing letters to people she knew at Hampton. She explained that Susan and her sister Marguerite would be excellent students to take on at the school.

At the Elizabeth Institute, Susan and Marguerite had been among white girls. Now they would be around African American and other Native American students. They would have a chance to learn about all kinds of people. Oh, there was one other thing. At Hampton, they would be going to school with *boys*.

That was the strangest part of all!

# 4.
# FOLLOWING
# A DREAM

Susan glided along, slowly at first, then a little faster, and then—

*Thud!*

She fell down hard. Her friend Walter laughed as he helped her up. He was teaching Susan how to ice-skate. Susan had walked and slid on ice before—but not with thin blades strapped onto her feet. It was a lot harder to keep her balance!

Susan was nineteen when she started at Hampton in the fall of 1884. She and Marguerite lived in a

**dormitory** called Winona Hall, where there were two or three girls to each room. Her day started bright and early, at five thirty a.m. First she did some exercises. Then she got dressed and ate breakfast, before reporting to her first class at eight forty. The next seven hours were packed with one class after another. There was writing composition, history, geography, philosophy, and literature. Susan also took classes in civil government, physics, biology, and art.

When the school day ended at three forty-five, Susan finally got a couple of hours of free time to relax before supper was served at six. At some boarding schools it was against the rules for students to talk at mealtimes, but not at Hampton. There the adults encouraged the students to have conversations—as long as the chatting and joking didn't get too loud!

Part of General Armstrong's approach to education was requiring his students to work. Under his guidance the boys learned things like carpentry and farming, while the girls mastered cooking, sewing, and other household skills. So two days a week Susan didn't go to class at all. Instead she dusted shelves and scrubbed floors. She washed and ironed clothes and helped with the cooking. Susan didn't mind the hard work. She'd been raised to get her hands dirty and do whatever chore needed to be done. Plus, at Hampton she even got paid a little bit. Susan decided to spend some of her money on piano lessons. That was educational. But she also couldn't resist buying some fabric to make new dresses.

Susan also joined several clubs. One was the **Temperance** Committee, whose purpose was to discourage drinking alcohol. Growing up, Susan had seen that alcohol could ruin people's lives, and she thought it was best if people didn't drink it. Another organization she got involved with was the Lend-a-Hand Club. Its members took on different projects to help people in the community. Charity and friendship were very important at Hampton. One year, when a tornado swept through the Omaha lands in Nebraska, a group of Sioux boys at Hampton took up a collection and donated the money to help the Omaha recover. Traditionally the Omaha and Sioux had been enemies, but at Hampton everyone was on the same side. They all learned to put aside their differences and depend on one another.

General Armstrong also focused on Christianity, and Susan joined a group of Christian students who got together to study the Bible and promote Christian ways. After church on Sunday mornings, Susan often made time to visit small, rural churches, where she taught Sunday school and read the Bible to the members.

One evening Susan found time to dash a letter off home. She wrote that she loved life at Hampton— but she missed her family. "The days are flying fast, but I want to see you all so much."[6]

Susan was excited as she finished up her supper. It was Saturday night, the second Saturday of the month—and that meant a special treat. Although boys and girls ate together, usually the boys went back to their own dormitory after the meal. But twice a month, on Saturday evenings after supper, the boys stayed longer. They joined the girls to play games like checkers, dominoes, and tenpins (bowling). If the weather was nice, there might be a game of tennis or croquet.

Susan hoped she would get to spend some time with TI. That was her nickname for a boy at Hampton, a Sioux Indian named Thomas Ikinicapi. At Hampton, Susan worked as a tutor, and TI was one of her students. TI had a background different from Susan's. He couldn't speak English very well, and he wasn't a good student. None of this bothered Susan at all. As they worked together over the months, Susan became very attached to him. He was sweet and kind. He had tousled hair and a face that always looked ready to break into a smile, and it didn't hurt that he was "the handsomest Indian I ever saw."[7]

Susan's sister Marguerite was dating another Sioux Indian, named Charles Picotte. The four of them—Susan, TI, Marguerite, and Charles—spent lots of time together.

In the spring of 1886, Susan graduated. She received a medal for her excellent grades and was chosen to give a speech at the graduation ceremony. After describing her early memories of growing up in Nebraska, Susan talked about how she admired white people and their civilization. She thanked the whites who had helped her get an education. Finally, she asked them to have patience as Indians worked to adapt to white culture. "Do not try to put us down, but help us to climb *higher*," she said. "Give us a chance."[8] Like her father, Joseph, Susan was proud of her Indian heritage—but, also like him, she believed that adapting to white culture was the best way forward.

Susan's family could not travel to see her graduate, but her friend Alice Fletcher was in the audience watching. Afterward Alice wrote a letter to the La Flesches to tell them about the event. Everyone "was delighted with her," Alice wrote. "I am so glad that she is to go forward in her grand career. She is I think the first Indian girl to advance so far."[9]

After two years at Hampton, Susan had far more formal education than most other Indians. She knew physiology, which is the study of how the body works. She knew geography, and she could talk about literature and art. She spoke four languages: English, Omaha, French, and Otoe (another Indian language). What came next for her? If she returned to the reservation, she could get married and raise a family. But Susan had bigger plans. She was interested in medicine—and she had the brains to be a doctor.

At the time, most people—men *and* women—did not think women were cut out for that job. It was hard, messy work. Supposedly women weren't smart enough or tough enough to handle it. But there were a few female doctors, and Susan was determined to be one of them.

In fact, the doctor at Hampton was a woman. Her name was Martha Waldron. Over the years, she and Susan had become friends. Martha had gone to school at the Woman's Medical College of Pennsylvania, in the city of Philadelphia. Martha suggested that Susan apply there.

Susan had not forgotten that terrible night so many years ago, when she had helplessly watched the Omaha woman die. If she could become a doctor and go back to the reservation, maybe she could do something good for her people. She took Martha's advice and applied to the college. Her teachers were pleased to write good recommendations for her, and everyone was happy when she was accepted.

But there was a big problem.

# 5.
# "IT IS SPLENDID"

Susan's face fell as she read the news. Throughout her time at Hampton, she had worked hard, and it had paid off. She'd gotten into the Woman's Medical College.

As it turned out, that wasn't enough. It wasn't bad grades or a lack of ambition holding her back. It wasn't even being a woman or being an Indian.

It was money.

The college cost much more than Susan and her family could afford. Susan had hoped she would receive a **scholarship**, but the school had already given out all its money to other students. It was discouraging, but Susan wasn't giving up—and neither was Alice Fletcher. When Alice heard about the setback, she went straight to work writing letters and asking for favors. She was used to solving problems. This one would not get the best of her!

Alice put Susan in touch with a woman named Sara Kinney, who was president of the Connecticut Indian Association (CIA). The CIA was part of a larger group called the Women's National Indian Association (WNIA). The members of the association were white women who had goals similar to General Armstrong's. They wanted to teach Indian women to practice Christian values and learn to fit into white society. Susan believed that was the way to succeed too. She hoped the CIA would help her.

Susan wrote a letter to Sara, explaining how she had wanted to be a doctor ever since she was a little girl. "Even then I saw the needs of my people for a good physician," she wrote. "I feel that as a physician I can do a great deal more than as a mere teacher, for the *home* is the foundation of all things for the Indians, and my work I hope will be chiefly in the homes of my people."[10]

When Sara Kinney read those words, she wanted to help. If Susan returned to the reservation after she finished school, she would be in a wonderful position to work with other Indian women. Sara's husband worked as a newspaper editor, and she got him to print an article about Susan and her goals, asking people to donate money to Susan's education. Meanwhile, Sara also convinced the government to contribute to Susan's expenses. Through these efforts, they raised the money. Susan was very grateful to the women she called her "Connecticut mothers."[11] Soon she was on her way to Philadelphia.

With a million people, Philadelphia was one of the biggest cities in the country. The houses were packed together in tight rows, their windows overlooking the ships that steamed constantly up and down the Delaware River. Newfangled electric streetcars clanged down the middle of the wide streets, with horses and carriages off to the sides. Wires strung between the tops of tall buildings brought power to the streetcars and streetlights. And people bustled among shops selling everything imaginable. When Susan entered her first department store, she could hardly believe how big it was. She counted eighteen rooms!

Unlike at Hampton, there were no dormitories at the Woman's Medical College. Instead Susan would now be more or less on her own. She rented a room at a boardinghouse near the college. It was more luxurious than anything she had ever seen before. Pretty pictures decorated the walls, and she had her very own washbasin, with a place to put her hairbrush and toothbrush. On the reservation, staying clean was a chore. Here she could wash her face every morning—and she got to wash her feet pretty often too. "I wish I could live like this at home," she wrote to her sister Rosalie.[12]

Still, Susan did feel a little out of place. The other women at the college wore silk dresses and fashionable kid gloves. Susan knew her ordinary calico dresses were much more practical than silk—and much cheaper!—but she wished they weren't so plain. And oh, how she wished she had a pair of gloves!

Soon after she arrived, the school's administrators threw a party to welcome the new students. Susan chose a blue flannel dress to wear. She still had no gloves to dress up the outfit, but then her landlady offered to lend her a pair. Susan gladly accepted, but they were too small and Susan accidentally ripped them when she tried them on. Fortunately, not having gloves didn't ruin her evening. As she made her way through the room, meeting many of the other 160 students at the college, she started to relax. Everyone was friendly and welcoming—and no one seemed to care that her hands were bare.

As the months went by, Susan got a little homesick, but mostly her classes kept her busy. She studied chemistry and physiology. She learned about the body's cells and tissues. Since it was a college for women, there was also a focus on **obstetrics**, the medicine involved with pregnancy and birth. Susan especially liked anatomy, which is the structure of the body. "Everything has a name," she wrote to Rosalie. "[Even] the little tiny holes in the bones. It is splendid."[13]

She described in detail how six students got to examine a dead body: two took the head, another two got the chest, and two more tackled the abdomen and legs. Bit by bit they peeled the skin away to show tissues, blood vessels, and bones. "I ... don't mind the dissecting room at all. We laugh and talk up there just as we do anywhere," she wrote to Rosalie. "I could tell you lots of things but I don't know as you would care to hear them."[14] None of it made Susan the least bit squeamish. She loved it all.

When she had a little free time, Susan enjoyed the city of Philadelphia. There was so much to do. If only she could figure out exactly *how* she was supposed to do it all. The streetcars were confusing! She would think a car was supposed to travel up one street, only to find out it traveled down a different street. Who could keep it all straight? Finally, though, after a few months of practice, Susan mastered the times and routes of the streetcar system.

Once she felt confident about how to get around, Susan went to art museums, operas, plays, and orchestra concerts. (Her favorite musicians were the mandolin players.) She might watch a parade or take a relaxing walk in the park, picking wildflowers or gathering pine cones.

She didn't have much money, but eventually she did have enough to be fitted for a dress that was fancier than the plain calico she had brought with her. "I've become a lady of fashion," she wrote to Rosalie. She also started to wear her hair in a bun, the way white women did, instead of in the long braids that were common among Omaha women.[15]

As Susan settled in, her classmates introduced her to some families in Philadelphia, and Susan often got invited into their homes. During one overnight visit, she was impressed that she got a bedroom all to herself, along with an ivory comb and brush to do her hair with. The next morning at breakfast, there were oranges to eat, and beside each person's plate was a small dish of water to rinse their sticky fingers in afterward. And she couldn't wait to tell Rosalie how her hostess had turned on a little faucet in order to serve coffee out of a silver pot.

The school, the city, her new life—it was *all* splendid.

# 6.
# DR. SUE

Susan stood among a group of medical students who had gathered to watch the doctor. He was dressed in a long white gown to protect his clothes, and his medical instruments were laid out neatly beside him. There were scalpels—special sharp knives used for surgery—and clamps and bandages. And there were a lot of towels, because there was going to be a lot of blood. The doctor was getting ready to perform an **amputation** on a patient.

Susan was one of the students who had come

from the Woman's Medical College. There was also a group of male students from the nearby Jefferson Medical College. The men stood on one side of the room, and the women stood on the other side. Both the men and the women had been looking forward to observing the surgery. However, some of the men did not think the women should be there and were teasing them about it. They thought the women were too delicate to watch the operation.

Were they strong enough to handle seeing all that blood?

Probably not, the men said.

Would one (or two) of them fall to the floor in a dead faint?

Probably so.

Susan had heard the talk, but she ignored it. She knew that some people would shudder and try to get out of the room, but she was excited. One day soon, she hoped, *she* would be the one standing at the operating table!

Then it was time for the surgery to begin. And after it did—sure enough, a student tumbled to the floor, sickened at the sight. It wasn't one of the female students, though. It was one of the men! Two of his classmates had to pick him up off the floor and take him out of the room. Susan thought that was pretty funny. Apparently the men were more delicate than the women. She couldn't wait to write home to Rosalie about what had happened. "I wasn't even thinking of fainting," she reported.[16]

Sarah Lockery grinned as she saw Susan coming up to her after chemistry class. She already knew what Susan wanted. She held out her notebook, and Susan gratefully took it. Susan loved the hands-on part of her studies, but sometimes the bookwork overwhelmed her. She found chemistry especially challenging. Fortunately, she'd met Sarah, an older student.

In some ways the two women were similar. For example, both were ambitious and devoted to their studies. In other ways they were different. For example, Sarah was a lot better at chemistry! Luckily for Susan, Sarah liked her and wanted to help. Sarah was happy to let Susan borrow her notes after class.

Exams were coming up, and there was a test almost every other day. Anatomy was Saturday. Physiology was Tuesday. And the dreaded chemistry was Thursday. Susan hoped she would pass everything, and she hit the books hard. Late into the night Susan and her classmates gathered in study groups so they could compare notes and quiz one another. It turned out that the tests weren't too bad. Afterward Susan was pleased that she'd studied all the right things for the anatomy exam, which she called "lovely."[17] Even the chemistry exam had been easier than she'd expected.

Having her exams out of the way was a relief, but Susan was still working hard all the time. Sometimes she felt a little numbness in her arms, or had some trouble breathing, but she didn't think it was serious. She was under a lot of stress, so it was probably normal for her body to react a little bit. It didn't keep her from taking classes in gymnastics and even weight lifting. The physical exercise was good for her—and she welcomed the chance to change out of her long skirts into knickers that fastened at the knee. They were much more comfortable!

As the winter holidays approached, Susan got excited. Her brother Francis was coming for a visit. She didn't have enough money to travel home, so it was the next best thing for family to come see her in Philadelphia. On New Year's Day, she and Francis decided to go to Independence Hall, where they could see the Liberty Bell, the original Declaration of Independence, and the US Constitution. There was a lot of history on display there.

But as they worked their way through the historic artifacts, Susan and Francis realized that something else was on display—them! People were staring at them. Even in a big city with lots of people, it was rare to see Native Americans. Susan and Francis felt very uncomfortable. "We attracted so much attention," she wrote to Rosalie afterward. "We concluded it was rather too hot in there and came out."[18] Once they were back outside, though, Susan and Francis just laughed about the incident.

One Christmas vacation Susan decided to go back to Hampton for a visit. Marguerite was still at school there—and so was TI. Susan missed them both.

Susan liked TI a lot, and it worried her teachers and her "Connecticut mothers." They all thought Susan had too much in front of her to be stuck on a boy, especially someone who was not as smart or ambitious as she was. It was very uncommon at the time for a career to be more important to a woman than marriage was, but everyone thought Susan was different. She had so much **potential** as a doctor. If she got married, her first obligation would be to her husband. It would hold her back. Everyone agreed that Susan needed to focus on school. Everyone except Susan, that is. She was still making up her mind.

Things did not go well during the visit to Hampton. Susan felt bad when TI spent time with other friends instead of her, and he was hurt when she paid attention to other people. Neither of them could figure out how to talk to each other. At one point Susan saw him looking at her with tears in his eyes. It made her want to cry too. "I felt so sorry for him," she wrote miserably to Rosalie.[19] When she left Hampton to go back to Philadelphia, TI couldn't even look at her. He buried his face in his handkerchief. Marguerite, who was watching the whole thing, broke down and cried.

Susan sensed that the relationship was over. She was sad, but she was also determined to make the best of it. Without a boyfriend, she could focus entirely on her education and career. And even though it was hard to let TI go, Susan wouldn't fall apart if she couldn't be with him. "It won't break my heart," she said in a letter to Rosalie. "I ain't made that way."[20]

At least her plans to be a doctor were on track. "I will be the dear little old maid we read of in books," she told her sister. "[I'll] come and see you all and doctor and dose you all. Won't that be fine?"[21]

*Dr. Sue.* She liked the sound of that.

That was what she would be. That was *who* she would be.

She had made up her mind.

# 7.
# MAKING HISTORY

Susan clutched a dollar tightly in her fist. She had made friends with several families in Philadelphia, and one of them had given her a dollar for spending money. A whole dollar, just for her! She could use it however she wanted. She remembered how much she'd wanted a pair of kid gloves when she'd first gotten to Philadelphia. She *still* wanted them. Now she could walk right into the store and buy some.

Then Susan had another idea. Christmas was

coming. Maybe she should find a few presents to send home to her family. She could save the dollar, of course. During her first summer break at the medical college, she'd run out of money and had had to go back to Hampton to work as a housekeeper. It would be nice not to have to do that again!

Or ... Or ... Or ...

There were dozens of ways she could spend that money, and it was hard to decide. Susan tucked the dollar away for safekeeping. She'd figure it out later.

Although Susan was used to her life in Philadelphia, she still missed her family terribly. She also felt bad that she wasn't at home to pitch in with the work, especially since her parents were getting older, and their health wasn't as good as it used to be.

After giving it some thought, though, Susan hit on a way she *could* help. She was a doctor, after all—well, *almost* a doctor. If someone at home needed medical advice, Susan was ready to offer it. She encouraged Rosalie to send her details about "as many cases as you can."[22]

The requests started coming. When Rosalie got pregnant, Susan told her not to work too hard. Instead she told her sister to get plenty of fresh air and sleep. When Rosalie's husband got sick, Susan prescribed taking less quinine—a common medicine that was used for various illnesses—and said he should focus on eating healthier foods.

Their father, Joseph, had to use a **prosthesis**—a wooden leg—because his leg had been amputated years before. When this wooden leg wore out, Susan took charge of ordering a new one. And when Rosalie reported that their mother, Mary, had developed sores on her feet, Susan sent a special ointment to help heal the sores, and instructions that her mother was not to walk around without shoes.

One day Susan opened a letter from Rosalie and

was especially alarmed. Their mother's feet had gotten much worse. Susan suspected that poor nutrition was part of the problem. Many Omaha did not understand that different foods provided different nutrients. Even when they did know about eating a balanced diet, they did not always have the money to buy what they needed. Susan thought her mother probably needed more protein to help her body get stronger and fight off the infection.

Then she thought of her dollar.

She dashed off a letter to Rosalie and put the dollar into the envelope. If Mary was better by the time the letter arrived, Susan said, Rosalie should use the dollar to buy their mother some meat, maybe chicken. But if Mary's condition had gotten worse, Rosalie should spend the money on a telegram to send word to Susan.

"I shall pray for her," Susan told her sister in the meantime. "Tell her all the time so she will be spared to us and we will all see each other again."[23]

Fortunately, Mary recovered. Susan did not get a new pair of gloves, but with that dollar, she'd given her family the best gift she could.

In the summer of 1888, almost two years after she'd started school at the Woman's Medical College, Susan finally got to go home. She happily threw herself into all the work that needed to be done. There was cooking and cleaning and sewing. There was stacking hay, caring for the horses, and measuring land to build fences. "A Western woman has to know how [to] do everything that [a] man does, besides her own work," Susan proudly wrote to her friend Sara Kinney.[24] There was one thing she refused to do, however. She was afraid of cows, and wouldn't go near them!

Susan had another very important job that summer, one that was much more difficult than any farm chore. A terrible measles **epidemic** had gripped the reservation, and Susan was one of the few people on the reservation with any medical training. She found herself busy caring for hundreds of sick people—and they weren't always cooperative!

More than one patient gave her a skeptical look after she prescribed medicine. Susan saw the questions on their faces: Why did she want them to take the white man's medicine? What if it didn't help? What if it made things worse?

*Patience*, Susan reminded herself. Even though she was frustrated, she had to have patience. Many Omaha had little experience with white men's ways. She couldn't blame them for not trusting medicine they didn't know anything about. On the other hand, if she was going to fight the measles epidemic, she had to find a way to convince her patients to let her help them.

She could tell them over and over that the medicine wouldn't hurt them. Or she could *show* them. That would be quicker, easier, and more likely to work! Susan spooned out some medicine and swallowed it as her patients watched. There! Nothing bad had happened to her. She'd proven the medicine was safe. That usually did the trick, and Susan could go to the next house.

That summer was exhausting. Some days Susan traveled twenty-five miles in a horse and buggy, which took several hours. Even so, she was still upset when she was able to visit "only" ten families in a day! In the end, eighty-seven people died, mostly children, but Susan had saved many more.[25]

When autumn came, Susan probably had mixed feelings about going back to Philadelphia. It was hard to leave home again, especially when she'd seen how much good she could do. But she knew she had to finish her education. Coming home for good would have to wait.

After several more months of school, Susan's graduation day finally arrived. She had been working toward this moment for three years. Susan was the **valedictorian**, which meant that she had the best grades of any of the thirty-six women in her class. Students at her old Hampton school had been following her progress. The newspaper at the school noted: "There is not much use trying to be as smart as she is, but I guess it wouldn't hurt us to try and be as good."[26]

Susan *was* smart and good, and she was one other thing: unique. On March 14, 1889, when she received her diploma, she made history. That piece of paper made her the first Native American in US history—male or female—to earn a medical degree.

# 8.
# NO COMPLAINTS

During the spring and summer of 1889, Susan worked as an **intern** for the Woman's Hospital of Philadelphia, where she assisted the main physician in charge. During the day she worked at the hospital, and in the evenings she often traveled into poor neighborhoods, making house calls.

Susan liked the work, but she still missed home. Her dream had been to become a doctor and then to use her skills to help the Omaha. She was waiting for the chance to make that happen. Then, one day, the perfect opportunity came up. She found out that the Omaha reservation school needed a doctor. Susan didn't waste any time. She got a pen and paper and started writing a letter to the person in charge of hiring—the US government's commissioner of Indian Affairs.

In her letter Susan explained that she was a fully qualified doctor. She pointed out how she was an Omaha herself, raised on the reservation. She knew the language and customs of her tribe better than any white person. She was the ideal person to take on the job as the reservation's school doctor. Who could argue with that?

Well, the commissioner certainly wasn't going to be the one to argue. He thought she was exactly right! By August the twenty-four-year-old Susan had a diploma, a job offer, and a ticket home.

Susan immediately got to work taking care of the students. She looked up their runny noses and down their sore throats and into their achy ears. She prescribed medicine when necessary, and never passed up the chance to explain that a good meal—and a good bath—could work wonders in keeping them healthy.

Her sister Marguerite taught at the school, and even though Susan had once said she didn't want to be a teacher, it was in her nature to help in any way she could. So when she was finished with doctoring for the day, she often sat down with the children to do schoolwork. She guided them through their math lessons and showed them how to write out the strange letters in their English spelling words. When the work was finished, she entertained them by telling folktales she remembered from her childhood and taught them to sing songs patriotic to the United States, like "America," also known as "My Country, 'Tis of Thee."

Susan was good at her job—maybe a little too good! When the students' parents saw what a good doctor she was, they started showing up at her door too. Susan got busier and busier. There was another doctor on the reservation who was supposed to be taking care of the adults, but he was white and did not speak Omaha. Many of the Indians did not trust him because he was an outsider. He struggled with the job, and a few months after Susan arrived, he gave up trying to compete with her and quit.

Susan jumped at the chance to take over for him, and she became the doctor for the whole reservation. It was home to 1,244 Omaha, spread across an area that was thirty miles long on one side by fifteen miles long on the other. (Some whites also lived on the reservation, but it was mostly Omaha.) That was a lot of ground to cover, and Susan was looking at a lot more work. She hoped she was ready.

In one of her first cases, a young mother visited Susan's office with her sick eight-year-old son. Susan examined him and prescribed some medicine, and then sent the two home. The boy hadn't been seriously ill, but Susan was still nervous. Would he begin feeling better? Had she done the right thing? She had to know.

The next day she saddled up her horse and rode the eight miles to the boy's home. As she approached, she saw him outside, happily playing in the creek. That was a relief. Soon, word spread about Susan's skills. "They fairly flocked in to me after that," she boasted.[27]

Everybody liked "Dr. Sue." Her office was filled with books and games for the children, and conversation for the adults. People didn't have to be sick to stop at her office—there were plenty of other reasons to pay a visit. They might ask for Susan's help in translating a letter into English. They might ask for her advice about money. They might confide in her about a family problem. Or they might just want to chat for a little while. Everyone could count on Susan's office being welcoming and friendly. There was just one hard-and-fast rule: no smoking!

Susan saw patients in her office when she could, but often she had to visit them in their homes. Usually she left home by seven or eight o'clock in the morning and did not return until nine or ten at night. If a patient lived nearby—within a mile or so—Susan would pack up her bag and just walk over. But walking was slow and tiring, so usually she rode her horse. It was a rough ride, though. The roads through the reservation were really just rough, bumpy dirt paths packed with rocks. More than once Susan bounced across the prairie and opened her bag to find a big mess of broken glass thermometers and bottles. Sometimes she rented a team of horses and a buggy, since two horses pulling a buggy made the ride smoother. But that was expensive, so Susan started saving up money to buy a horse team of her own. Then her trusted pair of horses, Pat and Pudge, took her everywhere she needed to go.

One time Susan's friend Sara Kinney, from the

Connecticut Indian Association, came to visit. When Sara asked what hours Susan worked, Susan laughed. "My office hours are any and all hours of day and night," she replied.[28] People could not always fit their need for a doctor into scheduled office hours. To Susan it didn't matter if it was three o'clock in the afternoon or three o'clock in the morning. She would be ready to help.

Even though Susan was a good doctor, she didn't make much money at her job. The salary was five hundred dollars per year, which was not much at the time. However, her friends in the Women's National Indian Association also asked Susan to act as a missionary, someone who spreads the Christian religion. Susan had been a faithful Christian her whole life, so she was a good choice. For this the WNIA paid her another two hundred fifty dollars per year. The WNIA also bought clothing and supplies that she needed for her practice. Even then, there wasn't always enough money. Many times Susan dipped into her own money to buy what her patients needed. Her work was often difficult, but she managed. "I have not a single thing to complain of," she wrote in a letter. "My life here is a very happy one."[29]

# 9.
# DOING HER DUTY

*Brrrr.* The thermometer read twenty degrees below zero, and the snow was blowing hard. It was a full-on Nebraska blizzard—brutal weather. Susan wished she could stay inside her warm house, snuggle under the blankets, and go back to sleep. But that was not how a doctor's life worked—especially not on the Omaha reservation.

Susan had gotten a message that someone needed her help, so she bundled up in her warmest clothes and wrapped a buffalo robe around her shoulders.

Then she stepped out into the biting wind and trudged through the deep snow to the barn to get the horses ready.

Hot or cold, rain or shine, Susan was used to going out in all kinds of weather to see her patients. Sometimes the illness was a common cold or a broken bone. Other times she was called to treat more serious things, like cases of influenza (flu), malaria, dysentery, cholera, or smallpox. Some of these diseases had come from European settlers. Indians had no **immunity** to them. An especially bad disease was tuberculosis, which attacked the lungs and was often fatal. It was also extremely contagious, caused by bacteria that spread through coughing and wheezing. Tuberculosis was a widespread problem in the late 1800s and early 1900s and was one of the most deadly diseases among Native Americans.

Susan had her hands full during the winter of 1891–1892. A flu epidemic on the reservation kept her away from home all day, making house calls to people who were too sick to come to her office. She left before the sun came up and did not return home until late at night. Then she fell into bed to get some sleep before getting up the next morning to do it all over again. From the fall of 1891 through the spring of 1892, she traveled hundreds of miles across the reservation, seeing more than 640 patients.

One evening a young man appeared at Susan's office door, desperate for help. He explained that his wife was gravely ill, and Susan promised to come the next day. When she arrived in the morning, Susan saw that the whole family was stuffed into a tiny one-room house. Her patient was lying on a pallet in the corner, sick with both flu and tuberculosis.

Although the house was neat and clean, Susan could see that the family was suffering. They were so poor, they did not have enough money to buy food. The sick woman had not eaten anything for four days. She did not even have enough strength to speak. "When I saw her I did not think she could live through the day," Susan recalled later.[30]

After making her patient as comfortable as possible, Susan went home. There she packed a bag with milk, eggs, and beef. Then she turned around and rode the six miles back to the sick woman's house, where she made dinner for the family. Susan knew the woman was too sick to recover and would soon die. But Susan didn't abandon her. For two weeks Susan traveled every single day to visit her— twice a day if she could. Some days she even stayed overnight. For the last two weeks of her life, the woman had a constant friend in Susan.

Another time, Susan paid a call to an elderly man who was also sick with flu. When she arrived at his home, she found him lying on the floor—sick, hungry, and completely alone. "No one was there to speak a word of sympathy even, to cheer him in his pain and loneliness," she remembered.[31] Susan started to cry when she saw how he was living—but her tears didn't last long. She had work to do. Under her care the man recovered.

Unfortunately, there just wasn't enough of her to go around. Susan was on the go more than seventy hours a week, and it was hard work. She had to travel miles through the bitterly cold weather, caring for desperately sick people. Her mind was always on getting to the next house, and the next house after that. There was always a next house.

Sometimes Susan could visit her sickest patients only once every few days, even though she wished she could check on them three times every day. One man told Susan that he was grateful for her attention but worried about her going out in terrible storms. He told her she shouldn't risk her own health. She should stay home if the weather was too bad. Susan appreciated his concern, but she didn't take his advice. "I told him I had to, for that was my duty," she said.[32]

That winter brought heartache to Susan personally too. She found out that Marguerite's husband,

Charles, was ill with tuberculosis. The family pitched in to do what they could. Susan used her doctoring skills. Charles's brother, Henry Picotte, came from his home in South Dakota to help out with the work. Unfortunately, Charles was too sick with the disease, and he died. Soon after, Susan received another piece of sad news. TI, the boy she'd liked at Hampton, had always been sickly, but now Susan learned that he had also died from tuberculosis.

Eventually the cold weather passed, and spring came. Susan was relieved when people began to get better. Now she turned her attention to keeping people healthy. She believed there was more to being a doctor than just curing sick people. She wanted to prevent them from getting sick in the first place. Susan told anyone who would listen that fresh air and sunshine were much better "medicines" than the kinds she poured out of little bottles. If the weather was nice enough, she encouraged people to open their windows while they were sleeping. She also taught the Omaha how to have good health habits by eating nutritious food, washing regularly, and keeping their homes clean.

Doctors and scientists were beginning to understand that germs cause diseases and that germs can be spread between people. But these discoveries weren't well known among most people. On the Omaha reservation it was common for people to eat from the same dishes, wash their hands in the same washbasins, and dry them on the same towels—even when they were sick. During an outbreak of conjunctivitis, a type of contagious eye infection, Susan cautioned people to stop sharing washbasins and towels. It was a simple solution—and it worked. After her warnings, the epidemic slowed down. Bit by bit Susan's efforts started to pay off. In a letter, she wrote: "I'm not accomplishing miracles, but I am beginning to see some . . . results."[33]

Some people would say Susan was too modest. She couldn't save every life, but she was saving some. To those people, she *was* accomplishing miracles.

# 10.
# BRIDGING
# A GAP

There would be art shows? Science exhibits? Cultural displays? Lectures by some of the world's most important people? If that was the case, Susan was definitely interested! When Alice Fletcher invited Susan to go to the World's Fair of 1893, being held in Chicago, Susan didn't hesitate to say yes.

It sounded like exactly the kind of thing she would enjoy. Thousands of people were expected to come, and it would be fun to be back in a big city—Chicago was even larger than Philadelphia! The fair was still a few months off, but that was okay. Susan was used to being patient. In the meantime she had plenty to keep her busy.

Part of Susan's work on the reservation was her job as a doctor. Another part was her role as a missionary. It wasn't unusual to see her attending church on Sunday morning as a member of the congregation, and then leading a service herself in the evening.

One time Susan found out about a young Omaha couple who were going to get married. The Omaha had their own wedding traditions, but Susan and her sister Marguerite convinced the couple to get married in the Christian church. The ceremony would be different from what the young couple were used to, but Susan didn't think there was too much that could go wrong. That was where *she* went wrong!

Susan had been raised to understand two very

different cultures. She had been born Omaha and was happy wearing a pair of moccasins and a buffalo robe, telling traditional stories around a fire at a powwow. But because of her time around white people at schools in the East, she was also perfectly comfortable discussing literature, in English, while wearing a fancy dress at the opera. That wasn't the case for most Omaha. For them, adapting to the strange customs of white men was difficult even if they wanted to—and they weren't at all sure they *did* want to.

The wedding did not go well. During the ceremony the minister asked the couple to hold hands. They gave him a strange look and refused. According to Omaha customs, that wasn't a proper thing to do. Then, after the couple exchanged vows, they had no idea what they were supposed to do next. They just stood there until the minister finally said, "You may go." So they did—the man down one aisle and the woman down another. Then they sat down on different sides of the church. It was awkward from start to finish.

Susan wasn't discouraged by one uncomfortable wedding, however. And while it was true that Indians didn't understand or like all of the white man's ways, she thought it was just as true that white men didn't understand Indians very well. Many whites still believed that Indians were inferior savages, stupid and violent. Susan spent hours writing articles for newspapers, trying to set the record straight. She believed both cultures had good things to offer, and wanted to bridge the gap between them.

Sometimes it seemed more like a canyon than a gap! Susan couldn't believe the kinds of things she had to explain. In one article, her irritation exploded onto the page: "Some ask the absurd question, 'Do the Indians really love their wives?'" The answer was yes! "The Indians are *human beings* just as the white people are."[34]

Yet although Susan sometimes got frustrated with

white people, she believed that Indians could—and *should*—learn from whites. That was the way to improve their lives.

"Give us a chance," she had said in her graduation speech at Hampton. By the early 1890s, Susan felt like the Omaha were doing just what they should. On the reservation, almost all the Omaha now lived in wooden houses, rather than in traditional earth lodges. A lot spoke English. Instead of wearing clothing made from buffalo skins, many now wore the cloth pants and dresses seen among white people. And as a tribe the Omaha had bought lots of new horses and equipment and were working to clear the land for farming. Susan thought it was all good progress. She hoped that in time the Omaha would be able to live as successfully as she believed white people did. Her goal was to help the tribe get there. When she wasn't doctoring, she translated documents, reviewed contracts, and gave advice.

Susan had a good reputation among the Omaha.

They thought she was smart and fair, and they trusted her judgment. Her door was always open. Best of all, they saw her as one of their own. When they needed someone who could speak for them in the white man's world, they came to Susan.

Susan's role in the Omaha community was important—and exhausting! She was devoted to her job and her people, but the work kept her constantly on the go. Susan had never been a particularly strong and robust woman. Now all her responsibilities were taking a toll on her health. Her head hurt. So did the back of her neck. And her ears.

In December 1892 the pain got so bad that she had to stop working and climb into her bed. She managed to get back to work early in 1893, but she had lost a lot of weight and felt weak. Riding all over the countryside tired her out. That spring, while she was out in a storm, she was thrown from her buggy. She was badly injured and had to go back to bed to recover again. Even worse, she had to tell Alice Fletcher that she wouldn't be able to go to the World's Fair.

Susan's mother was also ill. One day Susan got home to find Mary collapsed on the floor. She was barely alive. Susan was trying to take care of her mother, her patients, and herself. It was too much. In the fall of 1893, Susan wrote to the agent for the reservation and explained that she had to quit her job as reservation doctor. He did not want to let her go— she was too important! He tried to change her mind, but Susan stood firm. "She knew she would never regret it," Rosalie explained to their brother Francis in a letter.[35]

Susan loved her job, but she had reached her limit. Her days as the doctor of her people were over.

At least, they were for now.

# 11.
# A LANTERN IN THE WINDOW

It was true that Henry Picotte was handsome. He was also kind and friendly, and used polite manners. On top of all that, he had a good sense of humor and told funny stories.

Yes, there was plenty to like about Henry. But *marry* him? Marguerite could not believe what her sister was planning to do—and Marguerite had been married to Henry's brother Charles! The rest of the family was also shocked when Susan made her announcement. So were Susan's friends back in Philadelphia.

What was Susan thinking? She'd always said she would not get married, so that she could focus on her career. That was one reason why things hadn't worked out with TI. Of course, she had just quit her job, but that wasn't because she didn't *want* to work. It was because her health was bad. To her friends and family, that seemed like another reason *not* to get married. How could she be a good wife—maybe even a mother—when she was sick so often?

Some of Susan's friends thought Henry wasn't good enough for her. He wasn't educated and accomplished like she was. In fact, he had been a performer in a Wild West circus show. These traveling shows hired Indians to dress in robes and feathers and act like savage, uncivilized warriors—or worse. Henry, a Sioux Indian, had played the role of a strange creature: part man, part beast. Supposedly he'd been captured on a tropical island in Southeast Asia. His job was to sit, chained up, and growl at the spectators. All in all, it wasn't very respectable work. Even Susan later wrote that the two were "utterly unlike" each other.[36]

However, Henry had been out of the circus by the time Susan had met him in 1892. That was when he'd come to the Omaha reservation to help his brother Charles, who'd been ill with tuberculosis. Charles had died, but Henry had been there through it all. *That* was pretty respectable.

Anyway, Susan did not care what other people thought of Henry. She loved him, and he loved her. On June 30, 1894, they were married. Susan had celebrated her twenty-ninth birthday, and Henry was thirty-four. The newlyweds moved into a house in Bancroft, Nebraska, where they planted a garden of vegetables, an orchard of fruit trees, and bunches of flowers all around the house.

Now that Susan did not have the pressure of being the doctor for the whole reservation, she had more time to rest. Soon she was feeling better—and itching to go back to work. Henry was her love, but medicine was her life. She couldn't leave it for long.

While Henry worked as a farmer, Susan opened an office in their house and went into private practice. That meant she was in business for herself, rather than working for the Omaha agency. She could choose which patients to accept and which to turn down. Of course, Susan did not like to turn anyone down! She worked long hours to see as many people as she could. At night she placed a lantern in the window. The rays of light shone all night across the dark prairie, showing the way to Dr. Sue for anyone who needed her.

When her patients couldn't get to her, she went to them. One rainy night a telegraph came from a doctor in Lyons, a town nine miles away. The message was brief: "Find Dr. Picotte," it said. "Be quick."[37]

The telegraph operator scrawled out the message and went to get Susan. She loaded up her buggy and set out in the rain and dark. It was hard to see anything, but she made her way to Lyons by following a line of fence posts.

When she arrived, she found a woman struggling to deliver a baby. It was a difficult night, but by the morning both mother and child were doing fine. The local doctor noted that the happy ending was "thanks to the skill of Dr. Susan."[38]

In December 1895, Susan gave birth to a baby boy. The pregnancy had been hard on her, and she was grateful to have a healthy son. She and Henry named him Caryl. After Caryl was born, Susan did not think she had time to continue being a doctor. The Omaha people thought otherwise. When Susan said she could not make house calls because she could not leave Caryl, her patients told her to bring him with her. They didn't care if he cried or made a fuss. That was no excuse for Susan to stay home—and anyway, it was fun to have a baby around! So Susan bundled Caryl up and carried him in the back of the buggy as she made her rounds. It was an uncomfortable ride, though, and Susan hated bouncing Caryl around the prairie, so other times she left him at home with Henry, who was a devoted father. "Henry worships the baby," she wrote to a friend. "They are the greatest of friends."[39]

Even with Henry's help, being both a mother and a doctor was exhausting work. In 1897, Susan got sick again. Like before, the pain was mostly in her ears, but this was the worst it had ever been. She was so ill that her family thought she was going to die. Susan may have thought that herself. Many days she felt depressed, thinking that her work among the Omaha had not done any good. She had tried so hard to help her people, but she worried that they didn't know it. Maybe it had all been for nothing.

Bancroft was a small town, and Susan was a big personality in it. It didn't take long for the community to find out Susan was sick. *Did you hear about Dr. Sue?* One person spread the news to another. *It's awful. We've got to be there for her.*

Lying in her bed, Susan heard the front door open and close. She heard the voices of people talking, laughing, and praying for her. The house filled up with baskets of fresh fruit and vegetables, and bouquets of wildflowers picked from the prairie.

Visitors poked their heads into her room to check on her and then stayed to chat, sharing their stories of how Susan had helped them. Susan was moved by all the love and support coming her way. She *had* made a difference. She had been wrong to ever doubt it. Gradually she recovered. When she did, she wrote a letter to one of her old teachers, saying, "This summer taught me a lesson I hope I'll never forget."[40]

By 1898, Susan was feeling better and was staying busy with work. She and Henry welcomed their second child, another son, whom they named Pierre. Susan liked her life on the Omaha reservation, but it wasn't enough to satisfy her. Even though *she* was happy, all around her she saw people who weren't.

# 12.
# FIGHTING A TERRIBLE ENEMY

Susan had the attention of everyone in the room. They each held their breath, waiting for her to speak. Susan let them wait. The dramatic pause was part of her speech. She wanted to make sure everyone was listening—closely.

She'd already told some of the horrible stories. There was one about a man who had gotten drunk, fallen into the river, and drowned. Another story was about a man who froze to death. One who got run over by a train. One who was murdered by a friend who'd been drunk. These tragic events were part of a larger story. Alcoholism was killing the Omaha tribe. It was killing its traditions and its pride. One person at a time.

Alcoholism wasn't new among Indians or whites, but it hit the Indian community especially hard. When Susan's father, Joseph, had been chief, he had seen the problems it caused. Sometimes Indians would get drunk and get into fights. Other times they would spend so much money on liquor that they had none left to buy food and clothing.

Joseph had had no patience for this. "Whiskey makes us fools," he'd said bluntly. "We will have no more drink while Joseph lives."[41] His solution had been simple and harsh. First he'd declared alcohol illegal on the reservation. Then he'd created a police force of thirty men to enforce the law. Any Omaha who was caught drunk would get a public whipping. This traditional punishment was painful and humiliating. And it worked. After a few people suffered this severe treatment, the incidents of public drunkenness all but stopped. When Joseph died in 1888, however, the police force broke up. Within just a few years, the situation was out of control again.

Since the 1850s, the Omaha had surrendered most of their land to white men through various treaties. Now they were crammed onto a tiny fraction of the vast territory they'd once roamed freely. Some of them had received small plots of land in the allotment process, but overall that arrangement wasn't working well for them. They were used to managing land as a tribe, not as individuals. Plus, although they had experience raising a few crops for food, running large-scale farms was a different story. Much of the land just wasn't good for that.

They'd also had to give up their buffalo hunts. For one thing, the animals were becoming more and more scarce. In addition, the US government was pressuring many Native American tribes to stop these hunts, mostly because they wanted Indians to live more like white men did. The Omaha had held their last big hunt in the winter of 1876–77. All in all they missed their old ways of doing things, and it was making them bored and depressed. Desperate for some kind of relief, many turned to alcohol. And the white men were happy to sell it to them.

Susan had always been in favor of temperance, which meant drinking alcohol only in small amounts—if at all. As a doctor she tried to teach her patients how alcohol was bad for their bodies. And as a Christian she preached about its harmful moral effects on families. With her speeches she hoped to get through to her people and make them see the dangers of drinking.

Some Omaha resented her efforts. They wanted to be independent, and that included drinking if they wanted to. They told Susan to mind her own business. Susan didn't listen to them. In her mind, speaking out against alcohol *was* her business. Alcoholism was causing death among the Omaha, and her job was to keep the people alive. "I know that I shall be unpopular for a while with my people," she acknowledged. "But this is nothing, just so that I can help them for their own good."[42]

Susan was distressed that US government agents weren't doing very much to stop the flow of alcohol onto the reservation. She remembered a time as a child when her brother Francis had stood by and watched while some of his friends had bullied another boy. When Joseph had found out about the incident, he'd sternly told his son: "He who is present at a wrongdoing, and lifts not a hand to prevent it, is as guilty as the wrong-doers."[43] Susan felt like the same thing was happening now. To her, the problem was obvious, and the white men surely knew right from wrong. Sadly, she realized that many of them simply didn't care.

Susan did what she could to change things. She helped form a committee to find out who was bootlegging, which means selling alcohol illegally. Then she turned those names over to the agent for the reservation. It cost money to catch bootleggers, however, and when the money ran out, the bootleggers were back in business.

Susan also lobbied in favor of stricter **prohibition** laws that would make it illegal to sell alcohol on the reservation. However, when the time came to vote on the new laws, the whiskey-sellers were one step in front of her. Some of them had already gone out among the Omaha people and told them to vote against prohibition. Many Omaha still struggled to understand English, and they thought they were voting *against alcohol sales*. In fact, they were voting in favor of them!

Susan hated to see so many of her people hurting. It was a complicated problem, and no one could escape it entirely—not even Susan.

Henry was a loving husband, but he was also an alcoholic. He'd always liked to have a drink from time to time, and by the early 1900s he had started to drink more heavily. Perhaps he was depressed, or frustrated with how whites treated Indians. Perhaps he didn't realize that a little bit of drinking had turned into a lot. Whatever the reason, when he got sick with tuberculosis, his body was already run-down and damaged from alcohol. Tuberculosis was a serious disease even for someone who was otherwise healthy. Henry did not have the strength to fight it. Susan did her best to care for him, but in the end there was nothing she could do to save his life. He died in 1905, at forty-five years old.

Henry's death left a huge hole in Susan's life. She was heartbroken—and scared. She wrote to a friend that she could "almost go wild" with missing him.[44]

At only forty years old, Susan was also facing serious health issues. Even with her medical training, she didn't know what was causing the trouble with her ears, but it had made her go deaf in one ear. Now she was a widow with two young children to take care of. She didn't know how she could do it, but she didn't have much of a choice. It was all up to her.

# 13.
# ON HER OWN

Green, Susan decided. The house would be painted green.

It would have lots of windows.

It would have a big yard where Caryl and Pierre could play, and room for her mother, Mary.

And it would have a bathroom—an *indoor* bathroom.

As she stood on a piece of land in Walthill, Nebraska, one day in 1906, Susan saw all the possibilities. The property she'd bought was the perfect place to build a house.

*Her* house.

With Henry gone, she was working hard to create a new life for herself and her children. In her imagination Susan saw not only her house but her future.

One of the best things was that Marguerite would be living just across the street. After Charles had died, Marguerite had gotten married again, to a man named Walter Diddock. Walter and Susan got along well, and all their children were close. Susan was glad that Marguerite and Walter were going to build a house too. It would be nice to have family close by. Susan had to take care of her sons, her elderly mother, and any member of the Omaha tribe who happened to need a doctor. She could use all the help she could get!

It would take a while for the house to be built, though. In the meantime, Susan moved her family to Macy, Nebraska, a few miles away from her Bancroft home. Macy was where the Omaha agency was located. In fact, the town was named for the agency. "Ma" came from "O-*ma*-ha," and "cy" came from "agen-*cy*."

In Macy, Susan was offered a job as a missionary for the Presbyterian Church. She would still get to be a doctor, but she would also run church services and spread Christianity among the Omaha. Susan thought it was a good fit and happily said yes.

There was a lot of work to be done. When Susan first showed up for services at the local church, only a handful of people were sitting in the pews. Susan quickly took over and began holding services in the Omaha language. Word got around, and more people began to come. Within a few weeks, a couple dozen people were attending every week. After six months the attendance was up to almost a hundred. Susan was proud of her work at the church. She said she was the "pastor, janitor, organist and clerk."[45] She did whatever had to be done.

She was the same way with her house in Walthill. She kept a close eye on the construction and stayed involved in every decision. The wood had to be oak, she decided. The living room would take up most of the downstairs, so the carpenters needed to figure out a way to stick all the bedrooms upstairs. Whenever the builders came to work, Susan had something new to tell them.

Walter sometimes teased her about the shape of the house. Too tall! Too skinny! And what was up with that funny-shaped roof? Susan laughed along with him, but she didn't change her mind about anything. The house was just what she wanted.

Construction was finished in March 1908, and Susan and her family moved in. A wide front porch invited visitors to come inside. The windows—lots of windows—faced south, to let in fresh air during the summer, and as much sunshine as possible during the bleak Nebraska winters. The living room was large enough for Susan to hold meetings and parties. Bookcases filled with works of literature lined the room on three sides. A modern furnace provided heat, but there was also a large fireplace along the wall to help keep everything cozy. (It was also a good backup in case the furnace stopped working!) A rocking chair sat in front of the fireplace, and photographs lined the mantelpiece. Susan also hung a brass plaque on the mantel that read: EAST, WEST, HAME'S BEST. ("Hame" means "home.") There was even a telephone!

Marguerite and Walter were good neighbors. Sometimes Susan would drop by their house to eat breakfast on Sunday mornings, when Walter liked to make pancakes. Always acting like a doctor, Susan would scold her brother-in-law: "Walter, why make those doughy cakes?" she'd ask. "Can't you tell they will lie in your stomach like leather?"

Walter would just grin. He knew what was coming next.

Then Susan would sigh and say, "Fry me two or three."[46]

Susan still struggled to keep everyone on the reservation healthy. In 1909 there was an outbreak of diphtheria in Walthill. Diphtheria is a contagious infection that spreads through coughing and sneezing. Susan decided that the best way to keep the disease under control was to declare a **quarantine**. That meant that people could not leave their homes to go to school or work. They had to stay in until the outbreak was over. Susan was one of the few people who did *not* stay home. Instead she went door-to-door, checking on all the town's residents to make sure they were okay.

Slowly Susan adjusted to her new life. Rosalie had died in 1900, and Susette had died in 1903. She and Marguerite grew closer together. The two sisters threw themselves into the social life of Walthill. Both of them had gone through years of schooling around white people, so they were comfortable among both the Omaha and the whites who lived in the town. Susan taught Sunday school and joined a number of community organizations. She helped with fairs and fundraisers. A local lawyer let her use space in his offices to open a library. At home in her large living room, Susan hosted lectures and musical concerts. When she had time, she wrote articles for newspapers and magazines, describing Omaha traditions and legends.

As always, she did what she could to make life easier and more comfortable for her people. She made sure that a box of apples was delivered to Omaha children so that they had a treat on Christmas morning. She encouraged a seventeen-year-old boy to get an education. She prayed with a woman whose baby had died, and spoke at the funeral of a friend.

Business matters involving the Omaha tribe took a good chunk of her time. Many times the US government was late making payments it owed the Omaha as part of the treaty agreements they had signed years before. Again and again, Susan made phone calls and wrote letters to try to get the money sent. Every day she got letters from people who begged for her help. Every day brought something new.

Susan was frustrated. She knew that many Omaha

felt trapped by the rules of the white man's government, and she didn't blame them. She tried to help,
but sometimes it seemed she was not making much
of a difference. And then, one day early in 1910, a
group of Omaha paid her a visit.

They had a favor to ask.

# 14.
# "WE HAVE SUFFERED ENOUGH"

At first when Susan heard their request, she refused. Take a trip to Washington, DC, to talk to government officials? That was out of the question! She would have liked to be the person who stood up for the Omaha, but right now she didn't have the energy. She had all she could do just to keep herself going.

Susan was not feeling well again. She had seen a number of doctors to try to figure out what was wrong. At first they thought she had a disease called neurasthenia. The symptoms included headaches, chest pains, a racing heart, feeling tired all the time, and problems with digesting food. But nobody understood exactly what caused the disease, or how to cure it.

Susan told the group that she was sorry, but her health was too bad. She couldn't go to Washington. But she wasn't prepared for how the committee responded. They would not take no for an answer. Instead they gave her a choice: either she could go willingly or they would pick her up and put her on the train themselves!

Well, that wasn't much of a choice. Susan changed her answer to yes.

The Omaha were struggling with the US government over several issues. One was the location of the Omaha reservation agency. The Office of Indian Affairs wanted to close the Omaha agency and combine it with the agency for the Winnebago Indians, whose reservation was several miles north. Already some Omaha had to travel ten miles to reach their agency. If it was moved to the Winnebago reservation, the distance would double to twenty miles. Almost no one had a car, and twenty miles was a long way to walk or travel on horseback. That wasn't even the worst part. Susan suspected that the Omaha people would also have to do more paperwork and face more delays. A lot less would get done.

Susan decided to protest the decision. In a letter to her old friend Alice Fletcher, Susan wrote, "I should most certainly lose my self respect were I to keep still when I [thought] any thing was going to be done that would be to the **detriment** of the Omahas." And if the Office of Indian Affairs disapproved of her speaking up? "I don't care an **iota**!" she said.[47]

Another problem was the way the government handled the Omaha's money. The Indians were supposed to receive regular payments as part of the treaty agreements. However, US government officials often treated Indians as if they were irresponsible children.

They had to ask permission to get their own money, even when they wanted to spend it on simple, necessary items like a blanket or a wheelbarrow. Even worse was when people needed their money to pay for medical care. It could take months for the money to arrive. Sometimes it never came at all. Susan hated to see patients suffering because they couldn't afford treatment.

There was one other big thing at stake. It involved the land trusts the US government had issued to the Omaha back in 1884. The trusts had been written to last for twenty-five years, until 1909. During that time the Omaha had had to prove they were **competent** and able to manage their property. At the end of the twenty-five years, the US government was supposed to hold meetings to decide who was competent and who wasn't. (To be competent, someone had to speak English and be able to make a living.) Those who passed the test would get full control of their land. They could keep it or sell it if they wanted.

Then, just before the trust period ended, the government changed the terms of the deal. It added another ten years to the original trusts, even for people who could prove themselves to be competent.

Susan knew that some Indians still hadn't gotten used to handling money. The government hadn't given them much of a chance! She worried that if these Indians got control of their land, as the trusts had originally provided, the Indians would just turn around and sell it. More than likely, it would end up with **land speculator**s, who would pay much less than the property was worth. On the other hand, Susan didn't want to see Omaha who deserved to manage their land be forced to wait another ten years. They had earned the right to stand on their own. More and more, Susan believed the time had come for the Omaha to separate themselves from government meddling.

So in 1910 she traveled to Washington, DC, to meet with national officials. Susan was small and soft-spoken, but her words were powerful. "We are not stones—we are not driftwood. We have feelings, thoughts, hopes," she told them. "We have suffered enough from your experiments."[48]

In the end the national officials gave in. They agreed to hold the meetings to decide if the Omaha were competent. Unfortunately, things did not go well. Just as Susan had feared, some Omaha weren't ready to manage their land—or didn't want to. A lot of them didn't want to farm in the first place and had rented out their property. Now they sold it to white men who offered fast payment but low prices. Some Omaha ended up with nowhere to live. Susan hated to see people taken advantage of like that. And it made her sad to see the tribal lands slipping away. She knew that things couldn't stay the same forever, but she wished the Omaha were getting better prepared to face their future.

At home Susan was facing changes of a different kind. Henry had died five years before, but Susan had survived and made a new life for herself. Now Caryl and Pierre were older, and Susan felt her sons were ready for a more formal education. So far they had gone to school nearby, but now she enrolled them in a military school in Lincoln, Nebraska. It was about one hundred miles away. Susan missed having her boys around, and she took the train to visit them whenever she could grab the time, but that wasn't often. She was busier than ever.

As a doctor she still found herself fighting the same battles as when she'd first come back to the reservation. Diseases such as tuberculosis, smallpox, and influenza killed many people who should have had years left to live. Susan was a skilled doctor, but she was fighting an enormous battle. Often she did not see people until it was too late to save them.

One time, a young girl with tuberculosis came to Susan's office. The girl was much too sick for Susan to help. Not only did she die, but she spread the disease to her mother and grandmother. They died too. If only Susan had seen the girl in time, at least two people could have been saved. The sadness and frustration ate at her. She needed to reach more people. She needed to reach them sooner. What could she do?

Then she had an idea. One day Susan sat down and began to draw.

# 15.
# FOR EVERYONE'S GOOD

When she'd finished, the poster Susan had designed looked a little, well, *icky*. She had sketched pictures of houseflies nibbling on food, buzzing around a sick person, and crawling on a dead dog. Drawing such things was probably not how her art teacher at Hampton had expected Susan to use her talents! But pretty pictures of flowers or landscapes weren't going to save lives, and that was what Susan wanted to do.

She titled her poster "War Declared on the Fly."[49] Then she sent it out to women's clubs for them to hang up in meeting places, and she sent it to local newspapers to print. In the text, Susan explained how flies carried diseases that made humans ill. She showed people how to protect themselves by doing a few simple things, like covering their food. They shouldn't shut their windows all the time, because fresh air was important, but they *should* put screens in them. A flyswatter was a simple, effective tool—and so easy to make! (She provided instructions.)

Another of Susan's goals was to stop people from sharing dishes. Family members were always using the same plates and silverware without washing them in between. That was a sure way to get everyone in the household sick. But even worse than that were public drinking cups. That was a sure way to get everyone in the whole town sick!

In those days nobody carried around a plastic bottle of water. Instead they used public faucets. They could pour a drink of water into a cup that was kept nearby. Since everyone used the same cup, everyone got the same germs. The idea that germs caused diseases was not well understood then. Not everyone realized that sharing cups or other personal items was a problem. Susan knew it, though, and she was determined to stop it. She helped get a law passed that outlawed common cups. Stores began stocking disposable paper cups. Some places even installed drinking fountains, where the water spurted upward—no cup needed!

Susan also served as a member of Walthill's health board. She was strict. Store owners who broke the rules did not want to see her marching up to their doors. She inspected buildings and businesses, and if they were not clean, she didn't hesitate to make the owner pay a fine. Her efforts were similar to other public health programs happening in big cities in the East, such as in New York and Boston. But in Walthill, Susan was doing it almost all by herself.

Despite her efforts, not a day went by when Susan didn't hear about one of her people dying. For years she had treated patients in their homes, or in hers. Patients who were extremely ill might be transferred to a hospital in Sioux City, Iowa, about thirty miles to the north, or to a hospital in Omaha, Nebraska, which was about eighty miles to the south. Either one meant a long journey over bad roads. It was especially difficult and dangerous for someone who was ill.

Susan believed that what the Omaha really needed was a hospital of their own. They should be able to go to a place that was close to where they lived but had the modern facilities to treat more serious diseases or injuries. Maybe it was finally time.

Susan threw herself into this latest project. Day after day she wrote letters to the newspapers and to her friends in the East. She explained how a hospital would benefit the Omaha—especially children—and asked for money to help build it. She spoke in churches and at community meetings. She especially hoped that the Presbyterian Board of Home Missions would come through for her. They were the ones who had hired her to be a missionary to the Omaha after Henry had died. Surely they would see how important this was! She wrote to them, "We need a hospital more than anything else."[50]

Susan got what she wanted. The board gave eight thousand dollars to build the new hospital. Susan was thrilled. That was most of the ten-thousand-dollar budget! More donations came in. Another religious group, the Quakers, came up with five hundred dollars. A friend of Susan's who was a musician held a concert and donated a hundred dollars from the money he brought in. Word spread. Local churches and organizations chipped in to buy equipment and furniture for the hospital's **ward**s and rooms. And Marguerite and Walter donated an acre of land for the hospital to be built on.

The hospital opened on January 8, 1913. It had thirty-nine rooms. There were two general wards with six beds each. There were also five private wards (for people who wanted their own room). A maternity ward was set aside for mothers and babies. There was also an operating room, a kitchen, two bathrooms, and a reception area.

With her belief in fresh air and sunshine, Susan made sure every room had at least one window. The operating room had nine! A long porch gave patients a place to sit outside, where lilacs bloomed in the spring.

The hospital was located just five blocks from Susan's house. That made it much easier to get to work. Not at all like those days when she'd had to ride her horse for miles, crisscrossing thousands of acres on the reservation. The new hospital wasn't just for the Omaha, though. White people—and anyone else—could go there if they needed to.

It was open to everyone.

The hospital had been Susan's dream, but she worked there for only a short time. She was forced to cut back a lot on her work because her health was deteriorating badly, and fast. In particular, Susan had terrible pain in the bones of her face. Her doctors did not think she had neurasthenia anymore. Now they described her disease as "decay of the bone."[51] Today we believe that Susan most likely had bone cancer, an agonizing type of cancer that is difficult to treat.

As Susan lay in bed, exhausted and weak, her family looked everywhere for ways to help her. Then Susan's brother-in-law, Walter, thought he might have found one.

# 16.
# FINAL DAYS

The letter Walter wrote would have to travel overseas, almost five thousand miles, all the way to France. In it he described Susan's condition and asked for help. *Please*, he begged. The situation was urgent. Then he sealed the envelope and prayed that Susan could last long enough for that help to arrive.

The letter was going to a person so famous that she was known all over the world, even in rural Nebraska. Her name was Marie Curie. She was a scientist who had degrees in physics and math. With the help of her husband, Pierre, Marie had discovered a new **element** called radium. In 1903 the couple had even won a Nobel Prize for their research on radium. The Nobel Prize is one of the most important awards in science. Now Marie was interested in using her discoveries to help in medicine.

Radium gives off tiny, invisible pieces of **radioactive** material. Marie observed that these pieces were powerful enough to kill cancer cells. That was an amazing discovery. Maybe she'd found a way to cure cancer! Today we know that radioactive particles are extremely harmful to humans. Although doctors still sometimes use radium to treat certain types of cancer, it is used in very small amounts, for a short time. At the time, however, Marie and other scientists believed that radium could kill cancer without causing lasting damage to the patient.

Walter hoped Marie's theories were correct. In his letter he asked her to send some radium. Maybe it would help. By this time Susan could not get out of bed. She could barely eat. Her family came together to take care of her. Marguerite cooked her meals, and Marguerite's daughter brought them to Susan across the street. Caryl was home from school for the summer. Susan trusted only him to give her her medicines.

Sometimes she was not fully conscious and could not understand what her family was saying to her. But when she could understand, her family told Susan how much they loved her, and how much the Omaha people loved her. She had done so much for them. Susan was very humble when she answered. "I cannot see how any credit is due me," she said. "I am only thankful that I have been called and permitted to serve."[52]

In September 1915 a package from Paris arrived. Inside was a box with a small lump of radium. Walter's letter had worked! Immediately Susan's family contacted the doctor treating Susan and asked him to come. He arrived late that night and got straight to work, carefully inserting the radium into Susan's ear. It was difficult to maneuver, though, and he had trouble holding on to the small pellet. He accidentally dropped it, and it slipped far down into Susan's ear canal. Now the doctor had to get it back *out*. That took hours. Susan was in agony the whole time, and her family was in agony knowing what she was going through.

Over the years, they had seen Susan struggle with her disease. It had caused her so much pain. It had often kept her from the work she loved. More than once she had been so ill that they'd thought she would die. Would this be the time? Would Susan even wish to be alive if she couldn't live the life she wanted?

Maybe it was for the best that in the end the radium treatment did not work. Her family knew the fight was over and gathered around her bed. In the early morning hours of Saturday, September 18, 1915, Susan died. She was fifty years old.

The next morning, Sunday, the churches in Walthill were empty. Instead Susan's friends and neighbors were gathered at her house. Every room overflowed with the people whose lives she had touched over the years. They were the people she had nursed back to health, and the people she had comforted when even the best medical care could not save their loved ones.

At the funeral, three Presbyterian ministers spoke, praising Susan's work and her good character. Then, as the service drew to a close, another man stepped forward to speak.

He was an elder in the Omaha tribe, and he gave the final prayer in the Omaha language. It was a perfect way to honor Susan's memory. She was a woman who had learned English as a little girl but who'd never forgotten her native language.

She had spent her whole life speaking for her people.

# Epilogue
# AN ARROW TO THE FUTURE

In French, Susan's last name "La Flesche" means "arrow." That name fit her well. Over her fifty years, Susan shot her arrows with skill and care. She did not always hit her target, but she made a mark that can still be seen today. The lives of many Native Americans are better because of the work she did.

The newspaper at her Hampton school once described Susan as an "Arrow of the Future, [shot] from the bow of the Past."[53] Her past was the history of the Omaha people, the lives that her people had lived for generations before the arrival of white men. And her future was the new way of life that Native Americans had to adjust to in the late nineteenth century. Susan devoted herself to helping them make that adjustment. It was never an easy path to follow, but she did it with grace and intelligence.

The hospital Susan opened in 1913 closed a little more than thirty years later, in 1946. She was slowly forgotten. For decades there were just a few people who recognized her name. Then, in the early 1990s, an elementary school in Omaha, Nebraska, was named after her. The building in Walthill that housed her hospital became a National Historic Landmark. Once again her work is important to the Omaha people.

Susan's gravestone reads "Until the Day Dawns." Susan herself brought the dawn of one important day: the day when an Indian woman could become a doctor in the United States. In the 130 years since then, more Native American women have followed their dreams and become doctors as well.

Susan would have liked that. She worked all her life to help the Omaha people. She wanted them to succeed. For her, that was the dream come true.

# Glossary

**amputation** the surgical removal of a body part, such as an arm or a leg

**competent** able to do something properly

**detriment** injury or damage

**dormitory** a building where many people live, usually at a school

**eclectic** diverse, having a lot of variety

**element** one of Earth's most basic materials; all things are made from combinations of different elements

**epidemic** an outbreak of disease that spreads quickly and affects a lot of people all at once

**ethnologist** someone who studies different cultures and the ways they are alike or different

**etiquette** the manners to use and the ways to behave in various situations

**immunity** resistance to a disease

**intern** a person who is supervised as they work at a job in order to learn more about it

**iota** a tiny amount

**land allotments** individual pieces of land assigned to people

**land speculator** a person who buys land at low prices so they can later sell it for more money

**mission** an organization that provides sermons and services to promote Christianity

**obstetrics** a branch of medicine focused on pregnancy and childbirth

**potential** the ability to develop into something

**prejudice** a negative opinion of someone, without a good reason

**prohibition** the act of preventing the sale or distribution of alcohol

**prosthesis** an artificial limb, such as an arm or a leg, that replaces or improves a missing or injured one

**quarantine** the state of being in isolation, so as not to pass on a contagious disease

**radioactive** when something gives off particles of energy as it decays; sometimes the particles can be dangerous and toxic

**reservation** an area of public land set aside for American Indians to live on

**scholarship** a gift of money to pay for educational costs, typically given to the best students by a school, the government, or a private organization

**surrender** to give up something

**temperance** drinking alcohol in small amounts or not at all

**treaty** an agreement between two or more nations

**trust** an agreement under which property owned by one person is legally controlled by someone else, for the owner's benefit

**valedictorian** the student with the best grades in their graduating class

**ward** a section in a hospital, such as a maternity ward or a cancer ward

# Endnotes

1    Tong, *Susan La Flesche Picotte*, 56.

2    Green, *Iron Eye's Family*, 36.

3    Susan La Flesche, "My Childhood and Womanhood."

4    Pascale, "Healers," 74.

5    Pascale, "Healers," 74.

6    Tong, *Susan La Flesche Picotte*, 47.

7    Green, *Iron Eye's Family*, 134.

8    Susan La Flesche, "My Childhood and Womanhood."

9    Mathes, "Nineteenth-Century Physician and Reformer," 173.

10    Mathes, "Nineteenth-Century Physician and Reformer," 174–175.

11    Mathes, "Nineteenth-Century Physician and Reformer," 174.

12    Green, *Iron Eye's Family*, 139.

13    Mathes, "Nebraska's Indian Physician," 508.

14    Tong, *Susan La Flesche Picotte*, 73.

15    Pascale, "Healers," 74.

16    Mathes, "Nineteenth-Century Physician and Reformer," 176.

17    Mathes, "Nebraska's Indian Physician," 509.

18    Clark and Webb, "Susette and Susan La Flesche," 157.

19    Mathes, "Nebraska's Indian Physician," 517.

20    Green, *Iron Eye's Family*, 133.

21    Starita, *Warrior*, 140.

22    Tong, *Susan La Flesche Picotte*, 77.

23    Starita, *Warrior*, 130.

24    Tong, *Susan La Flesche Picotte*, 81.

25    Starita, *Warrior*, 145.

26    Starita, *Warrior*, 151.

27    Starita, *Warrior*, 162.

28    Pascale, "Healers," 75.

29    Mathes, "Nebraska's Indian Physician," 515.

30    Susan La Flesche, "My Work as Physician."

31    Starita, *Warrior*, 158.

32    Susan La Flesche, "My Work as Physician."

33    Pascale, "Healers," 75.

34    Susan La Flesche, "The Home Life of the Indian," 40.

35    Starita, *Warrior*, 189.

36    Tong, *Susan La Flesche Picotte*, 101.

37    Starita, *Warrior*, 216.

38    Green, *Iron Eye's Family*, 148.

39    Ferris, *Native American Doctor*, 65.

40    Mathes, "Nineteenth-Century Physician and Reformer," 179.

41    "Old Chief Joseph's Crusade," 275.

42    Starita, *Warrior*, 214.

43    Francis La Flesche, *The Middle Five*, 128.

44    Starita, *Warrior*, 221.

45    Tong, *Susan La Flesche Picotte*, 126.

46    Green, *Iron Eye's Family*, 153.

47    Tong, *Susan La Flesche Picotte*, 161.

48    Starita, *Warrior*, 251.

49    Tong, *Susan La Flesche Picotte*, 184.

50    Tong, *Susan La Flesche Picotte*, 187.

51    Mathes, "Nebraska's Indian Physician," 524.

52    Starita, *Warrior*, 273.

53    Green, *Iron Eye's Family*, 143.

# Bibliography

Clark, Jerry E., and Martha Ellen Webb. "Susette and Susan La Flesche: Reformer and Missionary." In *Being and Becoming Indian: Biographical Studies of North American Frontiers,* edited by James A. Clifton, 137–159. Prospect Heights, IL: Waveland Press, 1989.

Ferris, Jeri. *Native American Doctor: The Story of Susan LaFlesche Picotte.* Minneapolis: Carolrhoda Books, 1991.

Green, Norma Kidd. "Four Sisters: Daughters of Joseph LaFlesche." *Nebraska History* 45 (1964): 165–176.

Green, Norma Kidd. *Iron Eye's Family: The Children of Joseph La Flesche.* Lincoln, Nebraska: Johnsen Publishing, 1969.

La Flesche, Francis. *The Middle Five: Indian Schoolboys of the Omaha Tribe.* Madison: University of Wisconsin Press, 1963.

La Flesche, Francis. "Native American Public Intellectuals." In *Recovering Native American Writings in the Boarding School Press,* edited by Jacqueline Emery, 157–177. Lincoln: University of Nebraska Press, 2017.

La Flesche, Susan. "From Dr. Susan La Flesche." *The Indian's Friend* 2, no. 4 (December 1889): 2.

# BIBLIOGRAPHY

La Flesche, Susan. "The Home Life of the Indian." *The Indian's Friend* 4, no. 1 (June 1892): 39–40.

La Flesche, Susan. "My Childhood and Womanhood." *Southern Workman* 15, no. 7 (July 1886).

La Flesche, Susan. "My Work as Physician among My People." *Southern Workman* 21, no. 8 (August 1892).

Mathes, Valerie Sherer. "Susan LaFlesche Picotte, M.D.: Nineteenth-Century Physician and Reformer." *Great Plains Quarterly* 13, no. 3 (Summer 1993): 172–186.

Mathes, Valerie Sherer. "Susan La Flesche Picotte: Nebraska's Indian Physician, 1865–1915." *Nebraska History* 63 (1982): 502–530.

Morin, Karen M. "Postcolonialism and Native American Geographies: The Letters of Rosalie La Flesche Farley, 1896–1899." In *Frontiers of Femininity: A New Historical Geography of the Nineteenth-Century American West*, 168–195. Syracuse, NY: Syracuse University Press, 2008.

"Old Chief Joseph's Crusade." *The Friend* 82, no. 35 (March 4, 1909): 275.

Pascale, Jordan. "Healers." *Native Daughters* (special student magazine at University of Nebraska, Lincoln), 2010.

Picotte, Susan La Flesche. "Omahas and the New Order." *Omaha Daily Bee.* December 30, 1909.

Powell, Malea D. "Down by the River, or How Susan La Flesche Picotte Can Teach Us about Alliance as a Practice of Survivance." *College English* 67, no. 1 (September 2004): 38–60.

# BIBLIOGRAPHY

Pripas-Kapit, Sarah. "We Have Lived on Broken Promises." *Great Plains Quarterly* 35, no. 1 (Winter 2015): 51–78.

Seelye, James E. Jr., and Steven A. Littleton. *Voices of the American Indian Experience*. Santa Barbara, CA: Greenwood, 2013.

Starita, Joe. *A Warrior of the People*. New York: St. Martin's Press, 2016.

Tong, Benson. *Susan La Flesche Picotte, M.D.: Omaha Indian Leader and Reformer*. Norman: University of Oklahoma Press, 1999.

Welsch, Roger L. *Omaha Tribal Myths and Trickster Tales*. Athens: Ohio University Press, 1981.

# About the Author

**DIANE BAILEY** has written dozens of books for kids and teens, on everything from sports to science, but her very favorite topics are history and the people who made it. She also helps other authors by editing their books. When she's not working, she likes to take walks (really fast—try to keep up!), plant flowers (and hope they don't die), and watch scary movies (as long as they come out okay at the end). Diane has two grown sons and lives in Lawrence, Kansas.